May They All Be One

A Response of the House of Bishops of the Church of England to *Ut Unum Sint*

HOUSE OF BISHOPS OCCASIONAL PAPER

Church House Publishing
Church House
Great Smith Street
London SW1P 3NZ

ISBN 0 7151 5754 X

Published 1997 for the General Synod of the Church of England by Church House Publishing

Printed in England by Optichrome Ltd, Woking, Surrey

Contents

Foreword

Immediately after the publication of the Encyclical *Ut Unum Sint* we welcomed the call by Pope John Paul II to continue along a path towards the visible unity of the Church, 'which is difficult yet full of joy'. We promised a more considered response in due course to the issues raised in the Encyclical. In this response the House of Bishops of the Church of England reflects upon some of those issues. Disunity raises urgent questions which all Christians must address. It is Christ's will that all should be one for the sake of mission and because the Church is to reflect in its own life the unity and reconciliation God desires for all.

We thank God that in this century much progress has been made, although we recognize that there is still a long road to travel. It is a road we are travelling together – a road that we are confident will bring us to the goal of visible unity, the gift and calling of our Lord.

It is with this confidence that this response of the House of Bishops of the Church of England is made to the initiative of Pope John Paul II. It is made with the same joy and fraternal affection that characterizes the Encyclical itself. We trust that these reflections will be of help in the ongoing ecumenical dialogue.

On behalf of the House of Bishops of the Church of England

✠ GEORGE CANTUAR: ✠ DAVID EBOR:

June 1997

May They All Be One

A Response of the House of Bishops
of the Church of England to *Ut Unum Sint*

Introduction

1.   On 30 May 1995 the Archbishop of Canterbury and the Church of England's Council for Christian Unity responded immediately and warmly to the publication of Pope John Paul II's Encyclical *Ut Unum Sint*, which they recognized at once to be a major ecumenical contribution in our progress towards the full visible unity of the Church 'so that the world may believe' (see Appendix). At the same time they promised to give a more detailed response in due course after proper evaluation of the text.

2.   A number of informal reactions to the text have been published by members of the Church of England and by ecumenical groups in England. The present response has been formulated by the Faith and Order Advisory Group of the Council for Christian Unity at the request of the Archbishop of Canterbury. The members of the Faith and Order Advisory Group are appointed by the Archbishops of Canterbury and York. The Group brings together those who represent the various theological traditions found within the diversity of the Church of England. The response is offered as a contribution to the reception of the vision of the Encyclical and as a response to Pope John Paul's invitation to an ecumenical consideration of a world-wide ministry in the service of unity.[1] The opportunity is also taken to raise certain questions which we consider in need of further elucidation.

3.   In making this response we recognize the considerable achievements of the Anglican–Roman Catholic International dialogue (ARCIC). Both our churches have acknowledged significant areas of agreement in the Ministry and Eucharist texts of ARCIC I and notable convergence concerning authority. ARCIC II has continued the process, and its

reports, especially *Salvation and the Church* and *Church as Communion*, give further confidence that Anglicans and Roman Catholics do indeed have a profound unity at the level of faith. The report *Life in Christ* indicates that shared life requires agreement on morals as well as doctrine. It is on the basis of the mutual trust engendered by this important process that the Church of England accepts gladly Pope John Paul's invitation to respond to the insights of *Ut Unum Sint*.

4.   As the Papal Encyclical itself makes clear, any reflection on a ministry of unity, or on the unity of the Church itself, is a reflection on the mission of the Church. Mission belongs to the very nature of the Church, touching its unity, holiness, catholicity and apostolicity. As bishops, we are concerned about how the Church plays its part in God's mission. This involves asking not only questions about what the Church does, but also what the Church is and is called to be. What structures support Christians in the life and love of God, Father, Son and Holy Spirit? How do these structures unite and what are the qualities that are to inform their exercise? How should a world-wide ministry in the service of unity foster the unity of the Church, empowering and strengthening the whole Church in mission? Thus, questions of unity and mission are inseparable.

5.   Our response to *Ut Unum Sint* is shaped by our own Anglican experience of primacy. We understand primacy to be a particular form of the exercise of *episkope* (oversight). We are familiar with the exercise of primacy by a bishop who is called to lead in serving and caring for the people of God and to work with them in the oversight of the Church.[2] We experience the bishop as the chief pastor, who shares with his fellow bishops a special responsibility to maintain and further the unity of the Church, to uphold its discipline and to guard its faith. We have come to know the special role of primates in the provinces of the Anglican Communion, with the collegial exercise of a primatial ministry in the Primates' Meeting and now in the meetings of the Primates of the Porvoo Communion. We are also familiar with the special role of the Archbishop of Canterbury, 'a brother among brothers', within the Anglican Communion. His ministry is focused in his calling of the bishops to the Lambeth Conference and his presiding at that Conference. Arising from

this is his increasing pastoral and evangelistic ministry throughout the Communion.

6.   We recognize that we speak out of the experience of our particular historical relationships with the papacy. In England, as elsewhere in Europe, ecumenical relations are complicated and are often affected by the memory of the martyrs on both sides. This history remains deep within the memories of individuals and the corporate memory of the Church of England. The need to speak openly of this and to search together for a reconciliation of memories is crucial; otherwise the voice of reason and conscience will not be heard, present realities will not be admitted and the pilgrimage to full, visible unity will be impeded. We recognize with *Ut Unum Sint* that 'the commitment to ecumenism must be based upon the conversion of hearts and upon prayer which will also lead to the necessary purification of past memories'.[3]

7.   We speak, too, out of a context of being the established church in England with a particular relation to the State. The relation of churches to one another in this country is changing as we learn to worship and witness together. An important part of closer relations between ourselves and the Roman Catholic Church is the working closely together and also the mutual support of those who exercise a ministry of oversight. In every diocese, Roman Catholic and Anglican bishops, and those who exercise oversight in other churches, are beginning to share their ministry. Our response to *Ut Unum Sint* is conditioned by this experience, and this experience is one of the reasons why we believe that we are all profoundly affected by any change or development in the service of unity of the Bishop of Rome.

8.   We are aware that the response of the House of Bishops of the Church of England is only one Anglican response. We look forward to sharing it with other bishops of the Anglican Communion when we meet at the Lambeth Conference in 1998. We are clear that any developments in the exercise of the ministry of the Bishop of Rome in relation to the Church of England could not but affect the relationship with the whole Anglican Communion.

A welcome for the Encyclical

9.   The fact of the Encyclical is in itself a source of great joy. It express-
es the commitment of successive recent Popes and that of the Roman
Catholic Church,[4] especially since the Second Vatican Council, to the
ecumenical quest for the full visible unity of the Church.[5]

10. We note with appreciation the recognition that the ecumenical
movement had its origins largely among the churches of the
Reformation, with the early encouragement of the Ecumenical
Patriarchate.[6]

11. The document is important in a number of ways. We note that it is
addressed to all Christians, not just to Roman Catholics; to church leaders and theologians of other churches and ecclesial communities, as well
as to the bishops of the Roman Catholic Church.[7] We welcome this evi-
dence of the Pope's desire to make his ministry a service of unity to the
whole Church and accept gladly his invitation to reflect on the nature of
that ministry.[8]

12. We share the conviction that not only individual Christians but also
ecclesiastical 'structures' have been sinful[9] and that ecumenism requires
of all of us conversion and a change of heart. The Pope speaks for all
Christians in acknowledging, in the words of *Unitatis Redintegratio*, that
in many schisms 'people of both sides were to blame'.[10] At the same time
he asks forgiveness for his own office's responsibility for the 'painful rec-
ollections' which have made the papacy a difficulty for most other
Christians.[11] Quoting the Decree *Unitatis Redintegratio*, the Encyclical
refers to 'that continual reformation of which [the Church] always has
need'.[12] This corresponds closely to the conviction expressed in *The
Porvoo Common Statement*:

> The Church is a divine reality, holy and transcending present
> finite reality; at the same time, as a human institution, it shares
> the brokenness of human community in its ambiguity and frailty.
> The Church is always called to repentance, reform and renewal,
> and has constantly to depend on God's mercy and forgiveness.[13]

The Church of England shares this conviction of the peccability of every earthly institution and therefore recognizes its own need for reform and for penitence for the wrongs inflicted on Christians of other traditions.

13. We welcome the clear assertion that visible unity is God's will for the Church, and that this is not 'something added on'[14] but is integral to the nature of the Church[15] and its part in Christ's mission in worship, evangelization and service. *The Porvoo Common Statement* asserts that 'the Church, as communion, must be *seen* [emphasis ours] as instrumental to God's ultimate purpose. It exists for the glory of God to serve, in obedience to the mission of Christ, the reconciliation of humankind and of all creation (Eph. 1.10)'.[16] The visible unity of the Church is thus not an internal matter for the Christian churches themselves, but is a sign and instrument of God's will for the unity of divided humanity and of the whole of creation, to whom the Gospel of God's grace is addressed.[17]

14. Unity is not to be confused with uniformity. The Church of England has long had this vision of unity in legitimate diversity.[18] Such a vision requires a careful understanding of the source of unity in the nature and purposes of God and of the God-given diversity of human existence. It gives space for differences of cultural experience and expression, but it does not imply a disregard for those boundaries set by the once-for-all revelation of God in Jesus Christ. Of particular significance is the necessity for Christians to 'profess together the same truth about the Cross'.[19]

The faith and its formulations

15. The author of the Encyclical quotes his predecessor John XXIII's important distinction between the fundamental truths of the faith and the formulations by which they are expressed.[20] It has to be admitted that 'intolerant polemics and controversies have made incompatible assertions out of what was really the result of two different ways of looking at the same reality'.[21] This means that 'with regard to doctrinal formulations which differ from those normally in use in the community to which one belongs, it is certainly right to determine whether the words involved say the same thing'.[22]

16.   Our shared ecumenical methodology works with the notion that the same truths have been variously expressed in differing times and cultures; it recognizes both that our histories have given birth to emotive and polarized language, which has often played a large part in the continuing separation of our churches, and that our future lies in a generosity which willingly leaves behind the language of past polemics in the search for a common understanding in faith; it notes that the inexhaustible richness of the mystery of God not only permits, but also necessitates, different ways of looking at the same reality, of expressing that reality in the Church's life and worship. Thus, in evaluating the confessional statements of other churches and of ecumenical dialogues, it is not appropriate to demand exact verbal identity[23] with one's own familiar language, and it is appropriate to ask ourselves to listen to others' formulations and 'differing ways of looking at the same reality'. Such an approach enables separated Christians increasingly to move beyond their own 'partial readings'. It enables them to learn from each other and to grow in 'the faith of the Church through the ages'.[24] The Church of England continues strongly to endorse this shared ecumenical methodology, and seeks to employ it in its response to the Encyclical.

The teaching office of the Church

17.   Such ecumenical methodology does not undervalue the importance of doctrine and of the profession of the common apostolic faith. The Church needs to be able to speak authoritatively and with one voice, especially in areas where faith cannot admit divergence.[25] It needs appropriate organs through which to do so as it proclaims 'the faith uniquely revealed in the Holy Scriptures and set forth in the catholic creeds... afresh in each generation'.[26] In 1918 a committee set up by the Archbishops of Canterbury and York stated that:

> The Teaching Office of the Church is twofold. On the one hand the Church's function is to set forth the truth of the Divine revelation consummated in Christ, as contained in the Scripture, and as interpreted and evolved in the past. It has the duty of preserving and handing on to future generations a message of Divine origin and of transcendent importance for the wellbeing of the human

race. This message is variously described as the Gospel of Christ, the word of God, the Faith of the Church. On the other hand it has the duty of interpreting this gospel for each generation; of expressing it in the thought and language of the times, and in the light of advancing knowledge; and of presenting it to the world as a living faith. While the delivery of this message is the function of the whole Christian society, there has been from the beginning, and there is at the present time, a body of those definitely and officially appointed for carrying out this office as representatives of the Church. They are described as ministers of the Gospel, as ministers of Christ; and although the Teaching Office cannot and ought not to be confined to them it will largely depend upon their efficiency whether the Church is fulfilling its work properly.[27]

18.   Ecumenical consensus needs to be reached about the nature and exercise of the Church's teaching office and its competent organs. There is some unclarity about this in both the Roman Catholic and the Anglican traditions. This must be resolved if the Church is authentically and faithfully to fulfil the Lord's command[28] and to live in visible unity. In their responses to *The Final Report of ARCIC I*, Anglicans were able to endorse much of what the Commission said about this in its statements on Authority, both from the point of view of the understanding of authority and from that of the challenges this offers to our own practice. Resolution 8 of the 1988 Lambeth Conference summed this up in the following way:

> This Conference:

> Welcomes *Authority in the Church (I and II)* together with the *Elucidation*, as a firm basis for the direction and agenda of the continuing dialogue on authority and wishes to encourage ARCIC II to continue to explore the basis in Scripture and Tradition of the concept of a universal primacy, in conjunction with collegiality, as an instrument of unity, the character of such a primacy in practice, and to draw upon the experience of other Christian churches in exercising primacy, collegiality and conciliarity.[29]

19.   In responding to *Ut Unum Sint*, however, three areas are of particular and immediate concern with regard to the teaching office of the

Church. The first concerns what constitutes the Magisterium of the Roman Catholic Church. This involves issues concerning the relation of the Bishop of Rome to the collegiality of all the bishops, to the *sensus fidelium* and to the particular relationship of the Pope to the Curia.

20.   A second, and closely related, area concerns how the Magisterium is exercised. The Pope's own emphasis on his ministry as that of *servus servorum Dei* is crucial. We agree that this understanding is the best possible safeguard against the risk of separating power (and in particular the primacy) from service. This makes us suggest that the matter of ordinary and universal Magisterium needs consideration.

21.   A third question in the area of the teaching office of the Church concerns the understanding of the deposit of faith. The vocation of the Church 'to proclaim [the faith] afresh in each generation' constitutes a permanent obligation to interpret the original faith and witness of the apostles. The various expressions of Christian faith across the centuries and throughout the world today must always be seen to be consonant with this deposit, which also remains the Church's fundamental resource for addressing ever new questions posed in different ages and different cultures. As the *Elucidation* to ARCIC I's first statement on *Authority in the Church* expressed it:

> No endeavour of the Church to express the truth can add to the revelation already given. Moreover, since the Scriptures are the uniquely inspired witness to divine revelation, the Church's expression of that revelation must be tested by its consonance with Scripture. This does not mean simply repeating the words of Scripture, but also both delving into their deeper significance and unravelling their implications for Christian belief and practice. It is impossible to do this without resorting to current language and thought. Consequently the teaching of the Church will often be expressed in words that are different from the original text of Scripture without being alien to its meaning.[30]

In practice all churches work with an understanding of Scripture and Tradition and some principle of discrimination between those elements in the Tradition which are fundamental and those which are secondary.

Some clarification is needed, however, if divided churches are to be confident that they are confessing the faith of the Church through the ages, notwithstanding differences in formulation.

Decision making when churches are separated

22. Since the great divisions within the Church, it has rarely been possible for separated churches to speak together, and each church has in certain cases had to act as if the 'authority in Controversies of Faith'[31] belonged to itself alone. As the 1987 Bari agreed statement of the Roman Catholic – Orthodox International Commission puts it with reference to the East – West schism: 'After the schism occurred, East and West continued to develop, but they did so separately from one another. Thus it was no longer possible for them to take unanimous decisions that were valid for both of them.'[32]

23. In this process separated churches have sometimes taken decisions which have further deepened their divisions, and responsibility for church-dividing actions is widely shared. Examples can be seen in dogmatic definitions made by the Roman Catholic Church. Other churches, including the Church of England, have also made unilateral decisions on questions which many consider central matters of faith and order.

24. A closely associated question concerns the criteria and organs by which, when churches are separated, matters are deemed to be part of the deposit of the faith,[33] for example the 1994 declaration by the Congregation for the Doctrine of the Faith on the reservation of priestly ordination to men alone.[34]

25. When churches are divided, the principle and process of reception is still relevant to decisions taken by separated churches. This has as a precondition, however, that the churches already recognize one another. In the *Munich Statement* of the Roman Catholic–Orthodox dialogue it is envisaged that the principle of communion between local churches should be extended to 'sister Churches'.[35] 'Each must recognize in the others, through local particularities, the identity of the mystery of the Church.... It equally implies unity of witness and calls for the exercise of

fraternal correction in humility'.[36] Thus Pope John Paul's invitation in the Encyclical *Ut Unum Sint* implies a welcome recognition of the role other churches play in the discernment of God's will.

Full, visible unity

26. The Encyclical testifies to the remarkable achievements already made in the ecumenical movement. In particular, there has been an impressive convergence over the marks of full, visible unity. In the Encyclical there are different ways of presenting the dimensions of visible unity. For example, in paragraph 9 the Pope states that unity is constituted by the bonds of a profession of faith, the sacraments and hierarchical communion, whereas in paragraph 12 the list of the elements of sanctification and truth are described as including: the normative use of Holy Scripture, baptism, the sacraments including the Holy Eucharist, an episcopal ministry and devotion to the Virgin Mary. Many elements of this are in accordance with the Chicago–Lambeth Quadrilateral. The Church of England has recently set out the dimensions of full visible unity in the Porvoo, Meissen and Fetter Lane Common Statements. There is much common ground between the picture of unity in *Ut Unum Sint* and the growing consensus emerging more widely as a result of the efforts of the Faith and Order Commission of the World Council of Churches.[37] This consensus has also been clearly set out in the ARCIC II statement *Church as Communion*.[38]

Areas requiring further study

27. The Church of England welcomes the identification of certain areas requiring fuller study 'before a true consensus of faith can be achieved'. The Encyclical lists: (1) the relationship between Scripture and Tradition, (2) the Eucharist, (3) Ordination, (4) the Magisterium and (5) the Virgin Mary.[39] We note that ARCIC II is working on the first of this list. Already in the response of the Church of England to *The Final Report of ARCIC I*, the Church of England made clear that it considers the statements on the Eucharist and Ordination and their elucidations to be 'consonant in substance with the faith of the Church of England'.[40] In what follows we

comment further on the Magisterium and the place of the Virgin Mary. We go on to point to other issues which we consider also to be in need of further consideration as our two Communions move together.

The Magisterium

28. We agree that in the area of authority important questions still need agreement – especially, as noted above, concerning the exercise of the Magisterium. We consider a living teaching authority witnessing to and interpreting the faith 'uniquely revealed in the Holy Scriptures and set forth in the catholic creeds'[41] to be essential for the authentic proclamation of the gospel to each generation. We believe that this authority belongs to the body of the Church as a whole and that the discernment of the faith once delivered to the saints is a function of the whole body in which all the faithful in each particular church have a part to play at every level. Bishops with their synods have a particular responsibility for facilitating and guiding this process. Anglicans believe that their characteristic model of 'bishop-in-synod' embodies a conciliar principle whereby authority is exercised in a constitutional way.

29. It is to be regretted that the Encyclical makes so little reference to Ecumenical Councils and other conciliar forms of consultation and discernment in the Church. The *Valamo Statement*[42] describes synodal life as the principal form of practising communion among bishops during the history of the Church. As ARCIC I pointed out, a serious imbalance may occur when either primacy or conciliarity is emphasized at the expense of the other. This danger is increased when churches have been separated from one another. 'The *koinonia* of the churches requires that a proper balance be preserved between the two with the responsible participation of the whole people of God.'[43] In the Church of England and other Anglican churches the principle of conciliarity is firmly embedded in constitutional forms whereby bishops, clergy and laity all play a part in the governance of the Church at every level. Bishops retain a special authority in questions of doctrine and worship. The Church of England's response to ARCIC I underlined the need for this principle to be honoured and for more work to be done ecumenically both on the balance between

primacy and conciliarity, and on the role of the laity in the formation of the Church's decisions.[44]

30.   We are glad that the theme of authority is being studied together by our churches in the work of ARCIC II. We look forward to continuing the dialogue, especially concerning the relationships between the teaching authority of the Church and the People of God as a whole; between the universal Church and particular churches; between the Pope, the college of bishops and the Roman Curia; and between bishops and theologians.

The place of Mary

31.   The differences and misunderstandings between churches concerning the place of the Blessed Virgin Mary in Christian faith and devotion are closely related to the way in which authority is perceived and exercised in the Church.

32.   There is one mediator between God and man, Jesus Christ. Mary's place in Christian faith and devotion is determined by God's choice of her to be the Mother of our Lord and Saviour Jesus Christ. Therefore, in continuity with the faith of the ancient Church, and with the support of the Third Ecumenical Council, Anglicans acclaim Mary as Theotokos, and honour her place in the economy of salvation with special celebrations in the liturgical year.[45] She was prepared by divine grace for her role as mother of our Redeemer, by whom she was herself redeemed and received in glory in the communion of saints. Her song Magnificat is part of the daily common prayer of the Church of England. In devotion she is the model for all faithful and obedient disciples and thus for the Church herself. As in many parts of the Roman Catholic Church, for some Anglicans pilgrimages and other devotions are more important than for others. This variety is a strength within Anglican devotion.

33.   Anglicans, however, have reservations if and when high authority declares to belong to the most essential elements in the hierarchy of truths, beliefs or devotional practices that many believers do not see to be demanded by Holy Scripture or required by the biblically-rooted tradition inherited from the ancient Church.[46] We recognize that the honour of Mary and the saints attests in a special way the unique mediation of Jesus

Christ and the power of the gospel. We welcome the Pope's injunction 'not to impose any burden beyond that which is strictly necessary', and believe that his authority could be enhanced if this principle were seen to be applicable to this question.[47]

Implications of our common baptism

34. Potentially one of the most far-reaching assertions of the Second Vatican Council is the statement that:

> Whenever the sacrament of baptism is duly administered as our Lord instituted it, and is received with the right dispositions, a person is truly incorporated into the crucified and glorified Christ, and reborn to a sharing in the divine life.... Thus baptism establishes a sacramental bond of unity existing among all who have been reborn by it.[48]

The same point was made in *Baptism, Eucharist and Ministry (BEM)*: baptism 'unites the one baptized with Christ and with his people'[49] and, 'Through baptism, Christians are brought into union with Christ, with each other and with the Church of every time and place. Our common baptism, which unites us to Christ in faith, is thus a basic bond of unity.'[50] In a similar way, the present Encyclical recognizes that people enter the Body of Christ through baptism and the Pope states that the ecclesiological implications of this are far-reaching.[51] We too consider this to be a central ecclesiological and ecumenical question. If baptism is an act of God in his Church, and if people are baptized in divided churches, what does that say about the ecclesial status of the communities through which they are admitted to the community of salvation?[52]

35. In its response to *Baptism, Eucharist and Ministry*, the Church of England observed that:

> The growing consensus on baptism illustrates something of the unity which already exists between churches which remain in separation.... Where separated churches are able to acknowledge each others' profession of faith there is already a wide mutual recognition of baptism. This both presupposes and implies some

> mutual recognition of ecclesial reality, for it is within the context
> of the life of separated churches that candidates are baptised.[53]

Our recognition of the high degree of communion that exists between all the baptized, even when churches are divided, and the Encyclical's acknowledgement that 'the Sacrament of Baptism... represents a sacramental bond of unity linking all who have been reborn by means of it'[54] makes it all the more important that we explore jointly the theological, pastoral and ecumenical implications of this our common baptism for the Church's truly becoming 'a sign of that full communion... which will be expressed in the common celebration of the Eucharist'.[55] In particular, we must consider the implications of our common baptism in reference to the Decree *Unitatis Redintegratio* in both its asserting that 'the post-Reformation Communities lack that "fullness of unity... which should flow from Baptism"' and its observing 'that "especially because of the lack of the Sacrament of Orders they have not preserved the genuine and total reality of the Eucharistic mystery", even though "when they commemorate the Lord's Death and Resurrection in the Holy Supper, they profess that it signifies life in communion with Christ and they await his coming in glory"'.[56]

36. It is on the basis of the Church of England's recognition of the degree of communion that exists between all the baptized that we invite other baptized Christians to receive sacramental and pastoral ministrations from the clergy. *Ut Unum Sint* acknowledges that 'in specific cases and in particular circumstances, Catholics too can request these same sacraments from ministers of Churches in which these sacraments are valid'.[57]

37. We share Pope John Paul's joy at the extent to which, in particular circumstances, Roman Catholic ministers may offer the sacraments to other Christians.[58]

38. We observe, however, that the understanding of this openness varies considerably from place to place, as does also the recognition of the possibilities envisaged by the *Directory for the Application of Principles and Norms on Ecumenism.*

39. We note with sadness that the discipline of the Roman Catholic Church does not allow its members to receive the sacraments from Anglican priests.[59] We believe that urgent and serious consideration of this discipline is required in the light of developments since the publication of the Papal Bull *Apostolicae Curae* in 1896. The answer of the Archbishops of Canterbury and York, *Saepius Officio*, addressed the historical and theological issues raised by the Bull. Moreover, *The Final Report of ARCIC I* and the official responses of our two churches set the arguments of the Bull in a new context. We reaffirm our own commitment to the apostolic succession of the Church and to the interrelationship between the historic episcopal succession and the continuity of the whole Church in faithfulness to the original witness and teaching of the apostles.[60]

40. We recommend further exploration of the implication of the acceptance of each other's baptism for the recognition of ministries. We draw attention to some further words from the Church of England's Response to *BEM*: 'in as much as "baptism is normally administered by an ordained minister" (B 22), some would argue that such mutual recognition of baptism also implies a certain degree of ministerial acknowledgement'.[61]

Apostolicity and succession

41. We note that in paragraph 55 the Encyclical locates the 'kinship' between the Roman Catholic Church and the Eastern Orthodox Church (a 'sister Church') in the fact that 'although these Churches are separated from us, they possess the sacraments, above all – by apostolic succession – the priesthood and the eucharist, whereby they are still joined to us in a very close relationship'. The work of ARCIC and the official responses to *The Final Report of ARCIC I* reveal a similar 'kinship' between the Roman Catholic and Anglican churches.

42. The work of ARCIC has revealed 'substantial agreement' on the eucharist in the two areas which were once thought in the past to be causes of division and on the understanding of the priesthood of the ordained ministry. Further, the agreement on apostolic succession has

been underlined in the report of the House of Bishops, *Apostolicity and Succession.*[62] This report holds together the apostolicity of the whole people of God, living in fidelity to the teaching and mission of the apostles, and the 'effective sign' of that in the historic episcopal succession. It is worth quoting here our position as stated in *The Porvoo Common Statement*:

> In the consecration of a bishop the sign is effective in four ways: first it bears witness to the Church's trust in God's faithfulness to his people and in the promised presence of Christ with his Church, through the power of the Holy Spirit, to the end of time; secondly, it expresses the Church's intention to be faithful to God's initiative and gift, by living in the continuity of the apostolic faith and tradition; thirdly, the participation of a group of bishops in the laying on of hands signifies their and their churches' acceptance of the new bishop and so of the catholicity of the churches; fourthly, it transmits ministerial office and its authority in accordance with God's will and institution. Thus in the act of consecration a bishop receives the sign of divine approval and a permanent commission to lead his particular church in the common faith and apostolic life of all the churches.
>
> The continuity signified in the consecration of a bishop to episcopal ministry cannot be divorced from the continuity of life and witness of the diocese to which he is called.[63]

43.   The historic episcopal succession is not an optional extra in the life of the Church. It is a sign of God's promise to be with his Church and a sign of the Church's intention to be faithful to the teaching and mission of the apostles. While the Church of England hesitates, as *BEM* does, to use the language of 'guarantee' of historic episcopal succession, the House of Bishops nevertheless is clear that its understanding is not different from the one expressed by the Roman Catholic Church, as that is set out in its official response to *BEM*. When the Roman Catholic response makes use of the term 'guarantee', it clearly does not claim that the indefectibility, infallibility and apostolicity of the Church are unquestionably assured only by an historically demonstrable laying on of hands from the time of the apostles.

It follows that the word 'guarantee' should be understood in the context of a system of symbols and symbolic language. Symbols and symbolic language give and communicate meaning in complex and subtle ways. The historic episcopal succession is an expression first of Christ's faithfulness to the Church, second of the Church's intention to remain faithful to the apostles' teaching and mission. It is a means both of upholding that intention and of giving the faithful the confident assurance that the Church lives in continuity with the Lord's apostles and in anticipation of a glory yet to be fully disclosed.[64]

The role of the Bishop of Rome

44.   In dialogue between Roman Catholics and other Christians the role of the Bishop of Rome is already central. We are grateful for the Pope's admission that the exercise of his ministry is a question for all Christians.[65] Anglicans and Roman Catholics are at one in their understanding of the episcopate as a ministry involving not only oversight of each local church but also a care for the universal communion of which each church is a member.[66] ARCIC I sees the office of the universal primate as a special and particular case of this care for universal communion which is proper for the episcopal office itself. Anglicans are thus by no means opposed to the principle and practice of a personal ministry at the world level in the service of unity.[67] Indeed, increasingly their experience of the Anglican Communion is leading them to appreciate the proper need, alongside communal and collegial ministries, for a personal service of unity in the faith.

45.   Unity entails communion in faith and life. A world-wide ministry serving the unity of Church which has the Lord's promise that it cannot depart from the fundamental truth of the Gospel[68] must therefore have both doctrinal and disciplinary elements.

46.   As to doctrine and the controverted dogma of Papal Infallibility, we refer to our response to the ARCIC I statements on Authority in the Church for an extended comment.[69] At that time we wrote:

> We would wish to emphasise the importance of the discussion that needs to go on about the organs by which, under God, an all too human Church is preserved from fundamental error, and enabled despite all weaknesses and human failings to be the vehicle of the gospel of forgiveness and new life. It would be one thing for Anglicans to say 'yes' to the universal primacy of the bishop of Rome as the person who particularly signifies the unity and universality of the Church and to acknowledge his special responsibilities for maintaining unity in the truth and ordering things in love; it would be quite another to agree to infallibility without the understanding of reception as we have described it.[70]

47. In matters of discipline and the oversight of the communion of the Church we should not minimize the serious obstacles that still exist because of the present Roman Catholic understanding of the jurisdiction attributed to the primacy of the Bishop of Rome. The claim that the Bishop of Rome has by divine institution ordinary, immediate and universal jurisdiction[71] over the whole Church is seen by some as a threat to the integrity of the episcopal college and to the apostolic authority of the bishops, those brothers Peter was commanded to strengthen. This is not an argument for a primacy of honour only, or for the exclusion from a universal primacy of the authority necessary for a world-wide ministry in the service of unity. Although the question of jurisdiction is more difficult than the issue of primacy as such, ARCIC I and II and the international Roman Catholic–Orthodox dialogue have already made considerable progress, and we are confident that God will lead us to a proper common understanding and practice as the churches grow together.

48. Another major question concerns the necessity of visible communion with the Church of Rome and the Bishop of Rome as 'an essential requisite of full and visible communion'.[72] We have no difficulty in accepting the need for all churches to be in visible communion with each other, nor with the ancient understanding that the Church of Rome and the Bishop of Rome have a particular responsibility for expressing and safeguarding the unity of the Church. Nevertheless, the ministry of unity has manifestly not always ensured visible communion. Many individuals and communities share responsibility for the inability of the Church of

Rome to fulfil this ministry. Part of the remedy undoubtedly lies in a common exploration of the way in which the Church of the first millennium maintained her unity.[73] The bishops, successors of the Apostles, in communion with the Bishop of Rome, were central to the structures evolved both in East and West in reference to the apostolic heritage.

49.   The structure of the papacy as it has developed during the second millennium has been very different from the apostolic and patristic pattern, and we therefore welcome an approach which looks to our common heritage.

50.   At the same time, structures which evolved in and for the first millennium to serve the Church in God's mission cannot simply be re-created in the different circumstances on the eve of the third millennium. While being faithful to the past, we must also be faithful to the present context and the demands of common life, witness and service today. It is as we grow together in ecumenical fellowship that we shall be able to discern the appropriate structures of oversight at every level, including the question of communion with the Bishop of Rome.

51.   In this context we must point out that while the visible communion of the Church is essential if it is to be a credible sign of the unity God wills for all, the lack of visible communion, while weakening the life of divided churches, does not in itself destroy their essential reality, even in separation.

52.   We welcome the acknowledgement of the ecclesial reality of other communities expressed in *Ut Unum Sint* and look forward to further theological dialogue on the significance and implications of this acknowledgement.

53.   The relationship in both theory and practice between the Pope and the college of bishops is one particular area where we have already indicated a need for further investigation. This is not a purely Roman Catholic question, and many churches are currently discussing the interrelationship between primacy and collegiality. This is the subject of special studies in the Church of England and the Anglican Communion as a whole. It is closely related to another area of concern in modern Anglican ecclesiology, namely the relationship between the responsibilities possessed by a 'Province' for its own affairs and its responsibility

towards other Provinces and churches. It is widely recognized that within our Anglican Communion there is a danger that 'provincial autonomy' may be taken to mean 'independence'. Some consider that a primatial ministry with an appropriate collegial and conciliar structure is essential if this danger is to be avoided.

54. We note that the communion between the Roman Catholic Church and the Orthodox churches is described as almost complete despite the fact that the latter are not in visible communion with the Bishop of Rome.[74] In this context we recall some words of Cardinal Ratzinger:

> As far as the doctrine of the primacy is concerned, Rome must not require more of the East than was formulated and lived during the first millennium.... Reunion could take place on this basis: that for its part the East should renounce attacking the western development of the second millennium as heretical, and should accept the Catholic [sic] Church as legitimate and orthodox in the form which it has found through this development, while, for its part, the West should acknowledge the Church of the East as orthodox and legitimate in the form which it has maintained.[75]

Such an approach offers considerable hope, and could make possible a fresh consideration of many matters in which churches have developed in separation from one another.

'Real but imperfect communion'

55. We gladly accept that there is already a 'real but imperfect' communion between Christians and between ecclesial communities given in our common baptism.[76] This communion lacks the full visible expression which is its essential character. Hence we share with Pope John Paul an understanding that growth in visible unity and communion involves a process which may fittingly be described as 'unity by stages'. We look forward to discussing the implications of this process more deeply in relation to the celebration of the eucharist where churches are divided. The Encyclical reiterates the assertion of the Decree *Unitatis Redintegratio* that post-Reformation communities 'have not preserved the genuine and total reality of the Eucharistic Mystery', 'especially because of the lack of the

Sacrament of Orders'.[77] Our own church has always been careful to continue the ancient orders of the Church 'from the Apostles' time' and insists that the eucharist be celebrated only by those episcopally ordained priest.

56. In the continuing discussion, the verb *'subsistere in'*[78] as it is used here and in *Lumen Gentium* and *Unitatis Redintegratio* can be seen as being an ecumenical tool of great usefulness. We understand that it reveals an openness on the part of the Roman Catholic Church to the presence of elements of the one, holy, catholic and apostolic Church outside the bounds of the Roman Catholic communion. However, we note that the word has been interpreted in different ways both within the Roman Catholic Church and elsewhere, with commentators seeing it either as an inclusive or an exclusive expression. It therefore needs a common agreement between us on how it is to be understood.

57. The basic meaning of *subsistere* is 'to continue' or 'to remain'. The assertion of the Second Vatican Council that the unique Church of Jesus Christ 'subsists in the [Roman] Catholic Church'[79] is made on the understanding that all the elements of sanctification and truth can be found in the Roman Catholic Church. At the same time these elements are 'in a degree which varies from one to the other'[80] present in other churches and are the gifts of God and signs of his activity. They are a dynamic force for unity.[81] Among the separated communions 'in which catholic traditions and institutions continue to subsist the Anglican Communion occupies a special place'.[82]

58. If this implies a refusal by the Council simply to identify the one, holy, catholic and apostolic Church of the Creed with the Roman Catholic communion then the possibility is opened up for more substantial agreement about the nature of the Church, and more practically to positive steps towards mutual recognition. We too accept that the Church subsists in the Roman Catholic Church, but also believe that its subsisting is not exclusively confined to those under Roman obedience. In the Preface to the Declaration of Assent (Canon C 15) the Church of England describes itself as 'part of the One, Holy, Catholic and Apostolic Church'. If an exclusive interpretation of the phrase *'subsistit in'* is in fact the intention of the Council then a major ecumenical obstacle remains.

59.   We note, however, that the debate about how '*subsistit in*' is correctly to be understood is active within the Roman Catholic Church as well as between the churches, and we look forward to further development of the welcome possibilities it offers for a greater common understanding of the Church.

60.   Pope John Paul also speaks of the witness of the martyrs and their perfect communion in Christ even if the churches from which they come have not been visibly united.[83] He writes, 'I have already remarked... how an imperfect but real communion is preserved and is growing at many levels of ecclesial life. I now add that this communion is already perfect in what we all consider the highest point of the life of grace, *martyria* unto death, the truest communion possible with Christ who shed his Blood, and by that sacrifice brings near those who were once far off (cf. Eph. 2.13)'.[84] We consider all these points to have an importance yet to be fully explored in the future.

Conclusion

61.   We reiterate our welcome for the Encyclical *Ut Unum Sint* and express our own hope that the Pope's desire for his ministry to be a service of unity for all Christians be speedily realized. We offer our comments in the hope that the Pope and the leaders and members of other churches will be able to respond positively to the questions raised in this paper. The lack of unity among Christians contradicts the truth which Christians have the mission to spread and gravely damages their witness.[85] The division among Christians is a serious impediment to the work of Christ.[86] We welcome the insistence throughout the Encyclical on the inseparable relation between the mission and the unity of the Church. May God hasten the day when the *consensus fidelium* will truly accord to the one and only authentic *sensus fidei* and we shall all be one, so that the world may believe.

Appendix

Initial response of the Church Of England
to *Ut Unum Sint*

Issued on behalf of Lambeth Palace
and the Council for Christian Unity

1.   We welcome the Papal Encyclical *Ut Unum Sint*, with its reaffirmation of the ecumenical vision of the Second Vatican Council and its commitment to the goal of Christian Unity.

2.   At a time when there is growing impatience with the ecumenical movement and a tendency to give up on the search for visible unity, this urgent call by the Pope to continue along 'a path which is difficult yet full of joy' encourages us to continue with greater determination.

3.   There is much in the Encyclical with which Anglicans can agree wholeheartedly: the insistence on the primacy of common prayer; the need for repentance and conversion; the affirmation of what has been gained through joint action and patient theological dialogue; the recognition of our common baptism and the certain degree of communion that flows from it; and, not least of all, the conviction that unity is required for authentic mission.

4.   We pledge ourselves to face with the Roman Catholic Church those remaining matters of difference hinted at in the text. In particular, we look forward to exploring more deeply the ministry of unity which belongs to the Bishop of Rome, in the light of work currently being undertaken by the Second Anglican–Roman Catholic International Commission (ARCIC II).

5.   We look forward to making a considered response to the Encyclical and we encourage members of the Church of England to explore the text with their Roman Catholic brothers and sisters.

30 May 1995

Notes

1.   *Ut Unum Sint*, para. 96.

2.   Cf. The Ordinal in *The Alternative Service Book 1980*.

3.   Para. 2.

4.   It will be noticed that where the Encyclical refers to 'the Catholic Church', we have attempted to distinguish between the one, holy, catholic and apostolic Church of the Creeds (the Catholic Church) on the one hand, and the church (and particular churches) in full visible communion with the Church of Rome on the other (the Roman Catholic Church). The Catholic Church is the Body of Christ, a theological reality, created by God and participating in his own communion of love. It is not a 'denomination' or any other merely terrestrial institution. The marks and identity of this Church remain one of the underlying ecumenical questions. It will not, therefore, surprise anyone that while we are eager to discuss seriously all themes of theological importance, we are not willing to accept in advance any particular interpretation of the points at issue. An example of the ecumenical seriousness of this point may be seen in the Encyclical's statement that 'the Catholic Church thus affirms that during the two thousand years of her history she has been preserved in unity'. Our concern that unity should be fully visible makes it difficult for us simply to accept such a statement, as the divisions within the Church are painfully obvious to all.

For this reason, in this paper we continue our usual description of the church in communion with Rome as 'the Roman Catholic Church'. We are well aware that the Holy See has substantial ecclesiological reasons for preferring an alternative expression. Nevertheless, those reasons are themselves matters of ecumenical discussion. In the meantime, the assertion that 'the communion of the particular Churches with the Church of Rome, and of their Bishops with the Bishop of Rome, is – in God's plan – an essential requisite of full and visible communion', justifies the description 'Roman' and makes it inappropriate for other churches to accept the Roman Catholic Church's preferred usage.

5.   *Ut Unum Sint*, passim, but cf. especially paras 4, 5, 8 and 10.

6.   Para. 65.

7.   Paras 96, 101 and 103.

8.   Paras 94 and 96.

9.   Para. 34.

10.   Para. 11, cf. Second Vatican Council Decree on Ecumenism *Unitatis Redintegratio*, para. 3.

11.   Para. 88.

12. Para. 16, cf. *Unitatis Redintegratio*, para. 6.

13. *The Porvoo Common Statement* in *Together in Mission and Ministry: The Porvoo Common Statement with Essays on Church and Ministry in Northern Europe* (Church House Publishing, 1993), para. 20.

14. *Ut Unum Sint*, para. 9.

15. Cf. *The Porvoo Common Statement*, para. 21.

16. *The Porvoo Common Statement*, para. 18.

17. Cf. Archbishop Robert Runcie's opening address to the 1988 Lambeth Conference, *The Truth Shall Make You Free: The Lambeth Conference 1988* (ACC, 1988), pp. 11–24.

18. Cf. *Ut Unum Sint*, paras 50 and 54.

19. Para. 1; cf. Pope John Paul II, Address following the Way of the Cross on Good Friday, 1994: AAS, 87 (1995), 88.

20. Para. 81; cf. para. 38; *Unitatis Redintegratio*, para. 17; and the Joint International Commission for Theological Dialogue between the Roman Catholic and Orthodox Church, *Faith, Sacraments and the Unity of the Church* (Bari, 1987), paras 25–33.

21. *Ut Unum Sint*, para. 38.

22. Para. 38.

23. Cf. para. 38.

24. *Baptism, Eucharist and Ministry (BEM)* Faith and Order Paper No.111, WCC, 1982), Preface, p. 10.

25. Cf. ARCIC I, *The Final Report* (CTS/SPCK, 1982): *Ministry and Ordination*, para. 17.

26. *The Canons of the Church of England*, Canon C 15.1(1): Preface to the Declaration of Assent.

27. The Archbishops' First Committee of Enquiry, *The Teaching Office of the Church* (SPCK, 1918).

28. Matt. 28.20.

29. *The Truth Shall Make You Free*, p. 211.

30. ARCIC I, *The Final Report: Authority in the Church*, Elucidation 2. This corresponds closely to the assertion of the First Vatican Council that 'Neque enim Petri successoribus Spiritus sanctus promissus est, ut eo revelante novam doctrinam patefacerent, sed ut eo assistente traditam per apostolos revelationem seu fidei depositum sancte custodirent et fideliter exponerent' (*First Dogmatic Constitution on the Church of Christ*, ch. 4).

31. Thirty-nine Articles of Religion, Art. XX.

32. *Faith, Sacraments and the Unity of the Church*, para. 26.

33. Cf. the criteria for Councils to be recognized as 'Ecumenical' and the role of the Sacred Congregation for the Doctrine of the Faith (CDF) in declaring matters to belong to the deposit of faith.

34. CDF Responsum ad Dubium *Concerning the Teaching Contained in Ordinatio Sacerdotalis* (28 October 1995); cf. CDF Declaration *Inter Insigniores* (1976).

35. We recall with gladness Pope Paul VI's application of the term to the churches of the Anglican Communion. This gesture, like his giving of his episcopal ring to Archbishop Michael Ramsey, has been warmly received by Anglicans as a sign that their recognition of Roman Catholics as members of a sister church has been reciprocated.

36. Joint International Commission for Theological Dialogue between the Roman Catholic and Orthodox Church, *The Mystery of the Church and of the Eucharist in the Light of the Mystery of the Holy Trinity* (Munich, 1982), III(3)(b).

37. The Roman Catholic Church is a full member of the Faith and Order Commission.

38. ARCIC II, *Church as Communion* (CTS/CHP, 1991).

39. *Ut Unum Sint*, para. 79.

40. *The Church of England's Response to BEM and ARCIC: Supplementary Report to GS 661* (GS 747, 1986), para. 2(b); cf. Lambeth Conference Resolution 8.1 (*The Truth Shall Make You Free*, p. 211).

41. *The Canons of the Church of England*, Canon C 15.1(1): Preface to the Declaration of Assent.

42. Joint International Commission for Theological Dialogue between the Roman Catholic and Orthodox Church, *The Sacrament of Order in the Sacramental Structure of the Church with particular reference to the importance of Apostolic Succession for the Sanctification and Unity of the People of God* (Uusi Valamo, 1988), para. 52.

43. ARCIC I, *The Final Report: Authority in the Church I*, para. 22.

44. GS 747, para. 33.

45. The Council of Ephesus, 431.

46. ARCIC I, *The Final Report: Authority in the Church I*, para. 24(c).

47. *Ut Unum Sint*, para. 78; cf. Acts 15.28.

48. *Unitatis Redintegratio*, para. 22; cf. *Ut Unum Sint*, para. 66.

49. *BEM*: Baptism, para. 2.

50. *BEM*: Baptism, para. 6.

51. *Ut Unum Sint*, para. 66; cf. para. 42.

52. Cf. para. 84.

53. *Towards a Church of England Response to BEM and ARCIC* (GS 661, 1985), para. 43.

54. *Ut Unum Sint*, para. 66.

55. Para. 78.

56. Para. 67; cf. *Unitatis Redintegratio*, para. 22.

57. *Ut Unum Sint*, para. 46.

58. Ibid.

59. Cf. para. 46.

60. Cf. *Apostolicity and Succession*, House of Bishops Occasional Paper (GS Misc 432, 1994) and *The Porvoo Agreement: A Report by the House of Bishops* (GS 1156, 1995), para. 30: 'The House can only imagine entering into a relationship of visible unity with another church in England if that entailed a unity in faith, sacramental life, a single presbyteral ministry with a common episcopate in the historic succession and common structures: in short a single Church for the sake of strengthening a common mission and service to all.' It should also be noted that our recent agreement with the Nordic and Baltic Lutheran churches has enabled some churches which previously stood outside the historic episcopal succession to embrace this 'sign' of the Church's 'continuity in the whole of its life and mission, which reinforces its determination to manifest the permanent characteristics of the Church of the apostles' (*The Porvoo Common Statement*, para. 50).

61. *Towards a Church of England Response to BEM and ARCIC*, para. 43.

62. See note 60 above.

63. *The Porvoo Common Statement*, paras 48 and 49.

64. *Apostolicity and Succession*, para. 63.

65. *Ut Unum Sint*, paras 95 and 96.

66. ARCIC I, *The Final Report: Authority in the Church I*, para. 8.

67. Cf. *Towards a Church of England Response to BEM and ARCIC*, para. 238: 'Anglicans will find no difficulty in agreeing that... oversight of some kind ought to be exercised at a universal level'; and Resolution 8.3 of the 1988 Lambeth Conference: the Conference wished 'to encourage ARCIC II to con-

tinue to explore the basis in Scripture and Tradition of the concept of a universal primacy, in conjunction with collegiality, as an instrument of unity, the character of such a primacy in practice, and to draw on the experience of other Christian Churches in exercising primacy, collegiality and conciliarity' (*The Truth Shall Make You Free*, p. 211).

68. Matt. 16.18, Eph. 5.25–27.

69. *Towards a Church of England Response to BEM and ARCIC*, paras 233ff.

70. Ibid., para. 251.

71. First Vatican Council, *First Dogmatic Constitution on the Church of Christ*, ch. 3.

72. *Ut Unum Sint*, para. 97.

73. Para. 55.

74. Cf. *Unitatis Redintegratio*, paras 14ff.

75. J. Ratzinger, *Theologische Prinzipienlehre: Bausteine zur Fundamentaltheologie* (Munich, 1982), p. 209 (translated and quoted in Francis Sullivan, *Magisterium* (Dublin, 1983), p. 117).

76. *Ut Unum Sint*, para. 96; cf. paras 45, 46, 78 and 84.

77. Para. 67; cf. *Unitatis Redintegratio*, para. 22.

78. Second Vatican Council Dogmatic Constitution on the Church *Lumen Gentium*, para. 8; *Unitatis Redintegratio*, para. 13.

79. *Lumen Gentium*, para. 8.

80. *Ut Unum Sint*, para. 11.

81. Cf. ibid., para. 49, and *Lumen Gentium*, para. 8.

82. *Unitatis Redintegratio*, para. 13.

83. *Ut Unum Sint*, paras 1, 48 and 84.

84. Para. 84.

85. Para. 98.

86. Apostolic Exhortation *Evangelii Nuntiandi* (December 1975), 77.